AF478767

Soulful Shlokas For Kids

By Rekha Uday Amin

About The Book

As a child, I learnt shlokas and mantras from my father. They formed a part of my daily prayers. There is something magical about these beautiful pieces of spiritual poetry composed thousands of years ago. Even today, as an adult, I find that reciting these meaningful verses has a calming effect on me.

These shlokas and mantras are part of our rich heritage, and I wanted to share these treasures with our next generation. This compilation includes the importance, meaning, and gist of the shlokas so that our kids can comprehend the beauty of our power verses.

I hope that children will enjoy learning and reciting shlokas from this book!

*For my dearest Neil, who amazes
and inspires me everyday.*

Contents

Includes meaning and gist of shlokas

Early Morning Shloka

karaagre vasate Lakshmih

karamadhye Saraswati

karamoole tu Govindah

prabhaate karadarshanam

On waking up, rub your
palms, and place them on
your eyes.
Then slowly open your eyes,
look into your palms, and say
this shloka.

What does it mean? 

This shloka says that divinity lies in our hands- ***Goddess Lakshmi-****at the top,* ***Goddess Saraswati-*** *in the middle, and* ***Shree Krishna-****at the base. Every morning, we should look at our palms to get their blessings.*

— — —

The gist of this shloka is that we can earn wealth (through the blessings of Goddess Lakshmi), gain knowledge (through the blessings of Goddess Saraswati), and reach a balance between both (through the blessings of Shree Krishna) with our own efforts (use of hands).

Surya Vandana

Prayer to the Rising Sun

aadityasya namaskaram

ye kurvanti dine dine

janmaantarsahasreshu

daridryam nopajaayate

Face the rising sun
and chant this
shloka.

What does it mean? 

One who bows and prays to the Sun every day, will not face poverty even in 1000 births.

While Lighting the Prayer Lamp

shubham karoti kalyanam

arogyam dhana sampadah

shatru buddhi vinashaaya

deepa jyotir namostute

Take a bath and light the prayer lamp daily, both in the morning and evening.

What does it mean? 💡

I fold my hands and bow before the light that brings prosperity, auspiciousness, good health, abundance of wealth and destruction of the enemy's intellect.

Daily Prayer for Enlightenment

asatho mah sadgamaya

tamasomah jyotir gamaya

mrityormaamritam gamaya

om shantih shantih shantih

This is a prayer for self-actualization, seeking God to help you to be the best version of yourself.

What does it mean?

> *Lead me to truth from ignorance, lead me to light from the darkness, lead me to immortality from death. Let there be peace.*

Ganpati Vandana

Before any Auspicious Activity

vakratunda mahakaya

surya koti sama prabha

nirvighnam kuru me deva

sarva karyesu sarvada

Lord Ganesha's name is always invoked before any other God's name.
Say this mantra before starting any new activity, before a journey, before your exams and success will be yours.

What does it mean? 

Lord (Ganesha), who has a huge body, curved elephant trunk and whose brilliance is equal to billions of suns, may you always remove all obstacles from my endeavors.

Shloka to end every Prayer

tvameva mata cha pita tvameva

tvameva bandhuscha sakha tvameva

tvameva vidya dravinam tvameva

tvameva sarvam mama deva deva

kaayenavaacha manasendriyerva

budhyadmanava prakrite swabhavat

karomi yadyat sakalam parasmai

Narayanayeti samarpayami

Say this shloka at the end of your prayers. It expresses that God means everything to me and I surrender myself to God completely.

What does it mean? 

God, you are my mother, my father, my brother, and my friend.

You are my knowledge and my only wealth.

You are everything to me and the Supreme God.

Whatever I do with my mind, body, speech or with other senses of my body, Or with my intellect, I offer everything to the Lord Narayana.

Saraswati Vandana

Shlokas to begin your studies-1

saraswati namastubhyam

varade kaamaroopini

vidyaarambham karishyaami

siddhir bhavatu me sadaa

Before beginning your daily studies, say this prayer to gain Goddess Saraswati's blessings.

What does it mean? 

Shanti Mantra

Shlokas to begin your studies-2

om sahanaa vavatu

sahanau bhunaktu

saha veeryam karavaavahai

tejasvi naavadheetamastu

maa vidvishaavahai

om shantih shantih shantih

This mantra is to be jointly chanted by children and their teacher before beginning the day's study.

What does it mean? 

Om, May we all be protected

May we all be nourished

May we work together with great energy

May our intellect be sharpened

Let there be no animosity amongst us

May there be peace!

('we' in this mantra stands for students
and their teacher)

Hanuman Vandana

buddhir balam yasho dhairyam

nir bhayatvam arogata

ajatyam vak patutvam cha

Hanumat smaranat bhavet

Praying to Lord Hanuman makes us fearless and strong. If you are feeling scared or nervous, remember to chant this shloka.

What does it mean?

Intelligence, strength, fame, courage, fearlessness, good health, determination, and articulateness of speech, will all last forever if you pray to Lord Hanuman at all times.

Power Mantras

1. Gayatri Mantra

om bhur bhuvah swah

tat-savitur vareñyam

bhargo devasya dhīmahi

dhiyo yonah prachodayāt

Chant power mantras with complete devotion and focus, while seated in a prayer pose, with your eyes closed.

What does it mean? 

The Gayatri mantra is one of the oldest and most powerful of Sanskrit mantras. According to Swami Vivekananda, the meaning of this mantra: We meditate on the glory of that Supreme Being who has produced this universe; may He enlighten our minds

Power Mantras

2. Maha Mrityunjaya Mantra

om tryambakam yajamahe

sugandhim pushthivardhanam

urvaarukamiva bandhanaan

mrityormuksheeya maamritaat

This mantra gives us strength and is very beneficial during illness or when we are scared of something.

What does it mean? 

We worship the three-eyed one (Lord Shiva) who is fragrant, and who sustains all living beings. May he liberate us from death. May he lead us to immortality.

Guru Mantra 

gurur Brahma gurur Vishnu

gurur devo Maheshvaraha

gurur sakshat param brahma

tasmai shri gurave namahah

What does it mean? 

Guru is the representative of Brahma, Vishnu and Shiva. He creates(Brahma), sustains knowledge (Vishnu) and destroys the weeds of ignorance (Shiva). Guru is the supreme God and I salute and bow down to such a Guru.

Devi Mantra 

1

sarva mangala mangalye

Shive sarvaartha saadhike

sharanye trayambake Gauri

Narayani namosthute

 **What does it mean?**

You are the most auspicious of all, who fulfills all wishes of devotees, and who is the protector of all, with three eyes and a shining face. We bow to you, O Narayani.

Devi Mantra

2

ya devi sarva bhutesu shanti rupena sansitha

ya devi sarva bhutesu shakti rupena sansthita

ya devi sarva bhutesu matra rupena sansthita

namastasyai namastasyai namastasyai namo namaha

What does it mean?

Goddess Durga is omnipresent one. She is the personification of the Universal Mother. She is the embodiment of power, peace and intelligence in all beings. I worship her with all devotion so that she blesses me with happiness and prosperity.

More Meaningful Shlokas to remember

karmanye vadhika raste

ma phaleshu kadachana

ma karma phala he tur bhuh

ma te sangotsva karmanye

These divine lines (from the Bhagwad Gita) were said by Shree Krishna to Arjuna during the Kurukshetra war.

What does it mean? 

You have every right to work (action) but
do not expect fruits (results) out of it
Do not focus on the fruits and never be
inactive.

——— ——— ———

The gist of this is that one should focus
on the task at hand and do it as best
possible, and not focus on the rewards.
This single-minded focus allows one to
accomplish the task successfully without
any distraction.

More Meaningful Shlokas to remember

sukharthinah kuto vidya

vidyarthinah kuto sukham

sukhaarthi wa tyajet vidyam

vidyarthi wa tyajet sukham

 **What does it mean?**

If you pursue a life full of pleasures, you will not gain knowledge. If you are pursuing knowledge, you should give up the thought of a comfortable life. To gain knowledge, you have to toil.

More Meaningful Shlokas to remember

vidya dadati vinayam

vinaya dadati paatrataam

paatratva dhanamaapnoti

dhanaat dharmam tatatsukham

What does it mean?

Knowledge gives you discipline and humility. From discipline and humility comes worthiness and good character. From good character, one can gain wealth. By doing good deeds and charity with wealth, one can get happiness.

About the Author

Rekha lives by the motto: Do what you love.

An MBA by education, she has explored her passions (Management Consulting, Human Resource Management, German Language, Instructional Design, Mosaics, Blogging) and enjoyed varied roles (Senior Consultant, HR Officer, Mother) before rediscovering her primary love: Writing.

For this true-blue introvert, written words are the wings on which she flies. As a Content Strategist and Editor, she writes on varied creative and business topics.

You can contact her at connectwithrekha@gmail.com.